Twenty to Make

Mini Christmas Knits

Sue Stratford

Search Press

First published in Great Britain 2011

Search Press Limited
Wellwood, North Farm Road,
Tunbridge Wells, Kent TN2 3DR

Text copyright © Sue Stratford 2011

Photographs by Debbie Patterson at
Search Press Studios

Photographs and design copyright
© Search Press Ltd 2011

ISBN 978 1 84448 722 6

Suppliers

If you have difficulty in obtaining any of the
materials and equipment mentioned in this book,
then please visit the Search Press website for
details of suppliers: www.searchpress.com

Printed in Malaysia

Dedication
For Joe, Sam, Daisy, Poppy and Lola,
who enjoy Christmas nearly
as much as I do.

Contents

Introduction

I have had great fun designing these quirky Christmas knits. They are quick to knit and make full use of the selection of lovely yarns out there: soft and fluffy, sparkly and shiny; all perfect for little Christmas lovelies. As themed Christmas decorations are so popular, I have knitted two versions of every pattern. One is in traditional Christmas colours (red, green and gold) and the other in a more frosty colourway, showing how easy it is to get a completely different effect by varying the yarns.

The designs are all knitted using 4 ply yarn on small needles, ensuring that you get good detail. I used double-pointed knitting needles, as they are lovely and short for mini knitting, but they are not essential. Each design uses only a small amount of yarn and can be knitted quickly. However, make sure you take time when sewing them together, as a lot of the detail is achieved in the finishing.

You can use the mini knits as tree decorations, fasten them to a gift, or use them as table presents. I had a window display in my yarn shop last Christmas with a row of robins bobbing along on invisible thread, which looked fabulous. Some of the designs would make great toys.

Any tricky techniques are explained and they really help to make these little knits look extra special. Making any of these projects would be a great way to spend an evening when the nights start drawing in and Christmas is on the way.

Techniques

I-cord

To make an i-cord, cast on your stitches using a double-pointed needle, knit them and slide them to the other end of the same needle, then pull the yarn across the back of the needle and knit the stitches again. Repeat these instructions until the cord is long enough. By pulling the yarn behind the stitches on the needle, you close the 'gap' and give the appearance of French knitting. Alternatively, you can work the stitches in stocking stitch and sew up the seam.

Mattress stitch

This is a really neat way to join two pieces of stocking stitch together. The seam is practically invisible and not at all bulky. Begin by laying the work side by side with the right side facing you. Thread a darning needle with yarn and slip your needle through the horizontal bar between the first and second stitch of the first row on one piece and then repeat this process on the opposite piece. Work back and forth up this line of stitches for about 2.5cm (1in). Gently pull the yarn in the direction of the seam (upwards) and you will see the two sets of stitches join together. Repeat this process until you reach the top of the seam.

Wrap and turn

This technique ensures you do not end up with a 'hole' in your knitting when working short row shaping and turning your work mid row. Slip the following stitch from the left needle to the right needle. Move the yarn from the back to the front of the work, between the needles, and slip the stitch back to the left-hand needle. Turn the work.

Moss stitch

Row 1: (K1, P1) to end of row.

Row 2: (P1, K1) to end of row.

Therefore, on the second row you are purling the stitches you have knitted on Row 1 and knitting the stitches you have purled on Row 1.

French knots

Bring the needle up from the back of the work through to the front and wind the yarn around the needle twice. Take the needle through the work, half a stitch away, holding the loops around the needle with your finger while pulling the yarn through to the back of your work. Fasten off.

Blanket stitch

Thread a darning needle with yarn and bring to the front of your work about 1cm (³/₈in) from the edge. Leaving a small gap along the edge of the work, take the needle to the back of the work approximately 1cm (³/₈in) in from the edge and bring it back to the front at the edge of the knitting. Loop your yarn under the needle and pull it through until it lays neatly against the emerging yarn. Repeat this process.

Abbreviations

alt:	alternate
cm:	centimetres
dec:	decrease
foll:	following
GS:	garter stitch
inc:	increase
K:	knit
Kfb:	knit into the front and back of the stitch (increasing one stitch)
K2tog:	knit 2 stitches together
M:	marker
M1:	make a backwards loop on your needle by twisting the yarn towards you and slipping the resulting loop on to the right-hand needle. On the following row knit or purl through the back of the st.
P:	purl
PM:	place marker
P2tog:	purl 2 stitches together
psso:	pass slipped stitch over
rem:	remaining
rep:	repeat

RS:	right side
skpo:	slip 1, knit 1, pass slipped stitch over
sl:	slip a stitch
SM:	slip marker from left to right needle
SS:	stocking stitch
ssk:	slip 2 sts knitwise one at a time, pass the two slipped sts back to left needle, knit both together through the back of the loop
ssp:	slip 2 sts knitwise one at a time, pass two slipped sts back to left needle, purl two slipped sts together from the back, left to right
st(s):	stitch(es)
tbl:	through the back of the loop
tog:	together
W&T:	wrap and turn (see opposite)
WS:	wrong side
YO:	yarn over needle, resulting in another stitch

Making up

All the mini knits are sewn together using a darning needle and the same yarn the item has been knitted in. If any other needles (e.g. a sewing needle) are required, they are shown on the individual patterns.

The charts for the motifs for the Nordic Bunting on pages 46–47.

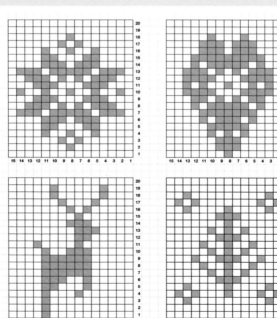

Twinkling Star

Materials:
Gold 4 ply yarn
Sequin yarn
Spare needle/stitch holder
Toy filling

Needles:
1 pair 3.25mm (UK 10, US 3)
  knitting needles

Measurements:
Approx. 8cm (3¹⁄₈in) across from point to point

Instructions:

Star points (make five):
Holding a strand of gold 4 ply yarn and a strand of sequin yarn together, cast on 2 sts and K 2 rows.

Next row: K1, M1, K1 (3 sts).

K 2 rows.

Next row: K1, K1fb, K1 (4 sts).

K 1 row.

Next row: K2, M1, K2 (5 sts).

K 1 row.

Next row: K2, K1fb, K2 (6 sts).

Place sts of each point on a spare needle or stitch holder.

Centre of star:
With RS facing, K across all five points of the star (30 sts).

Next row: (K1, K2tog) to end of row (20 sts).

K1 row.

Next row: K2tog to end of row (10 sts).

K1 row.

Thread yarn through rem sts and draw up, fasten off and sew side seam of star.

Make a second star shape in the same way.

Making up:
With WS together, sew the stars carefully together, folding all the loose ends into the inside of the star and stuffing gently with toy filling as you go.

8

Starry Night

Make other stars in silver and you have a starry firmament of Christmas decorations for the tree or around the house.

Christmas Tree

Materials:

Green 4 ply yarn
Small amount of red 4 ply yarn
Red beads
Small brass bell
Toy filling
Green sewing thread and sewing needle

Needles:

1 pair 2.75mm (UK 12, US 2)
 knitting needles

Opposite
White Christmas
This alternative tree is made
from sparkly white and silver
4 ply yarn, clear beads and a
star button for a shimmering,
snowy feel.

Measurements:

Approx. 9cm (3½in) tall

Instructions:

Tree (make two):

Using green yarn, cast on 3 sts.
K 1 row.
Work inc rows as follows:
K1, M1, K to last st, M1, K1 (5 sts).
K 1 row.
Rep these 2 rows three more times (11 sts).
Cast off 3 sts at the beginning of the next 2 rows
(5 sts).
Next row: K1, M1, K to last st, M1, K1 (7 sts).
K 1 row.
Rep the last 2 rows four more times (15 sts).
Cast off 4 sts at the beg of the next 2 rows (7 sts).
Next row: K1, M1, K to last st, M1, K1 (9 sts).
K 1 row.
Rep the last 2 rows five more times (19 sts).
Cast off all sts.

Trunk:

Using red yarn, cast on 10 sts and work 2cm (¾in)
in SS. Cast off.

Making up:

Place the two tree shapes together and sew
them together, stuffing them lightly with toy
filling as you go. Fold the trunk in half and
attach it to the base of the tree. Sew on beads
using a sewing needle and green thread. Use
the picture as a guide. Attach the bell to the
top of the tree.

Gingerbread Heart

Materials:

Beige 4 ply yarn

Small amount of red 4 ply yarn

Red felt or a button

Spare needle/stitch holder

Toy filling

Needles:

1 pair 3.25mm (UK 10, US 3)
   knitting needles

Measurements:

Approx. 7cm (2¾in) from
   top to point of heart
   (excluding hanging cord)

Instructions:

Heart shape (make two):

* Cast on 3 sts and P 1 row.

Row 2: K1, M1, K1, M1, K1 (5 sts).

Row 3: P.

Row 4: K1, M1, K2, M1, K2 (7 sts).

Cut yarn and place sts on a spare needle or st holder.

Rep instructions from * to make a second 'top' to your heart. Do not cut yarn.

Place both pieces of knitting on the same needle with WS facing.

Next row: P across both pieces (14 sts).

Work 2 rows in SS.

Next row: K2tog, K to last 2 sts, ssk (12 sts).

P 1 row.

Rep the last 2 rows a further four times until 4 sts rem.

Next row: K2tog, ssk (2 sts).

Next row: P2tog and fasten off rem st.

Making up:

Place the hearts with wrong sides together and using a darning needle and beige yarn, sew the hearts neatly together, gently stuffing with toy filling as you go. Using red 4 ply yarn, blanket stitch around the edges of the heart (see page 6). Attach a red felt heart or a button in the centre of the heart with a cross stitch in beige yarn. Repeat on the other side. Make a hanging cord by twisting two strands of yarn together, one beige and one red. Attach the cord to the top of the heart.

Opposite
Sparkling Heart
The alternative features
shimmering white and
pale blue yarn and a
mother of pearl heart
button in the centre.

Tiny Sweater

Materials:
Red 4 ply yarn
Spare needle/stitch holder

Needles:
1 pair 2.75mm (UK 12, US 2)
    knitting needles
Cable needle

Measurements:
Approx. 5.5cm (2¼in) tall

Abbreviations:
C4B: Place the next 2 sts on a cable needle
    and hold at back of work, K2, K2 sts from
    cable needle.

C4F: Place the next 2 sts on a cable needle
    and hold at front of work, K2, K2 sts from
    cable needle.

Instructions:

Body of sweater (make 2):
Cast on 18 sts.
Work 2 rows of rib as follows:
K1, P1, to end of row.
Cable pattern:
Row 1: K.
Row 2: P.
Row 3: K5, C4B, C4F, K5.
Row 4: P.
Rep these 4 rows four more times.
Next row: Cast off 5 sts, K across the foll 8 sts
and place on a st holder or spare needle, cast
off rem 5 sts.

Sleeves (make 2):
Cast on 8 sts and work 2 rows in K1, P1 rib.
Work 4 rows in SS.
Next row: K1, M1, K to last st, M1, K1 (10 sts).
P 1 row.
Work a further 4 rows in SS.
Cast off and fasten off yarn.

Making up:
With RS facing, K across 16 held sts for the
front and back of the sweater. Work in K1, P1
rib for 10 rows. Cast off in rib. Sew the shoulder
seams and collar seams of the sweater. Sew
the sleeves in place and sew up the sleeve and
body seams. Fold over the rib neck.

Opposite
Good Wool at Christmas
These miniature sweaters make great tree
decorations or comical table presents, and
they don't take nearly as long to knit as the
full-sized version!

Mini Mittens

Materials:

4 ply self-patterning sock yarn
Toy filling

Needles:

1 pair 3.25mm (UK 10, US 3)
   knitting needles
Spare needle

Measurements:

Approx. 6cm (2³⁄₈in) from cuff to
   fingertips with cuff folded over

Instructions:

Mitten (make two):

Cast on 20 sts and work 12 rows of K1, P1 rib.

Next row: K9, PM, K2, PM, K9. The sts between
the markers will form the thumb.

P 1 row. You are now working in SS.

Next row: K to M, SM, M1, K to M, M1, SM, K to
end of row (22 sts).

P 1 row.

Rep the last 2 rows until you have 8 sts between
the markers (26sts).

Next row: K9, remove marker, K across 8 sts of
thumb, turn (remove 2nd marker). You will now
be working just on the thumb sts.

Work 3 rows in SS.

Next row: K2tog, rep to end of row (4 sts).

Fasten off yarn.

With RS facing, rejoin yarn to the second half
of the mitten and knit the 9 sts to the end of
the row.

P 1 row and work across all 18 sts of mitten.

Work a further 2 rows in SS.

Next row: ssk, K5, K2tog, ssk, K5, K2tog (14 sts).

P 1 row.

Next row: ssk, K3, K2tog, ssk, K3, K2tog (10 sts).

P 1 row.

Next row: ssk, K1, K2tog, ssk, K1, K2tog (6 sts).

P 1 row.

Cast off rem sts.

Cord:

To make the cord, twist a double length of yarn
until it twists on itself. Alternatively, plait three
lengths of yarn.

Making up:

Sew the side seam of the thumb and then sew
the side seam of the mitten, bearing in mind
that the cuff will be folded back over the mitten
and the WS of the cuff will show. Sew the cord
into the tops of the mittens inside the folded
cuff. Stuff a little toy filling into each mitten.

Pink Perfection

Gloves on strings take us right back to childhood winters, so these make a fun decoration or gift – perhaps for someone who always loses his or her gloves! The alternatives are knitted in soft pink and cream yarns.

Christmas Mouse

Materials:

Cream 4 ply yarn
Pale pink 4 ply yarn
2 beads for eyes
White sewing cotton
Sewing needle
Toy filling

Needles:

1 pair 3.25mm (UK 10, US 3) knitting needles, (double-pointed needles recommended)

Measurements: Approx. 7cm (2¾in) tall

Instructions:

Mouse body:

Using cream yarn, cast on 6 sts and work 6 rows in GS.

Next row: Cast on 6, K8, (Kfb) twice, K2 (14 sts).

Next row: Cast on 6 sts and K all sts (20 sts).

Next row: K9, (Kfb) twice, K9 (22 sts).

K 2 rows.

Next row: K2tog at each end of the row (20 sts).

K 1 row.

Next row: (K2tog, K7) twice, K2tog (17 sts).

K 2 rows.

K2tog at each end of the next row, K 2 rows.
Rep from * to * until 11 sts rem.

K2tog at each end of the next row, K 1 row,
rep from * to * until 3 sts rem.

Next row: sl1, K2tog, psso, fasten off yarn.

Ears (make 2):

Using cream yarn, cast on 4 sts in MC and K 1 row.

Next row: K2, M1, K2 (5 sts).

K 1 row.

Next row: K2, Kfb, K2 (6 sts).

Next row: K1, K2tog twice, K1 (4 sts).

Next row: K2tog twice (2 sts).

Next row: K2tog and fasten off yarn.

Ear linings (make 2):

Cast on 3 sts using pink yarn and work 3 rows in SS.

Next row: sl1, P2tog, psso. Fasten off rem st.

Arms (make 2):

Using cream yarn, cast on 4 sts and work an i-cord (see page 6) 2.5cm (1in) long. Thread yarn through sts, pull up tightly to gather and fasten off yarn.

Tail:

Using cream yarn, cast on 4 sts and make an i-cord approx. 5cm (2in) long.

Making up:

Sew up the seam on the front of the mouse, and the nose will automatically curl over. If the nose seems too long, sew a thread up inside the body to the end of the nose and then back down again, pulling as you go to shorten the nose. Stuff with toy filling and sew up the base, easing in as you go. Sew the ear linings to the ears and attach the ears. Attach the arms and tail. Embroider the nose using pink yarn. Using a sewing needle and white sewing cotton, sew on beads for eyes and make whiskers by looping backwards and forwards through the nose. Cut the whiskers to the required length.

'Twas the Night Before Christmas...

Either of these mice would look great around your house at Christmas time, looking poised to grab any festive leftovers. The alternative is made from sparkly white yarn.

Fairy Mouse

Materials:

Pink 4 ply yarn

Small amounts of fine cream yarn and silver lurex 4 ply yarn

Fine wire

Star-shaped button

Knitted Christmas Mouse (page 18)

Sewing needle

Measurements:

Approx. 7cm (2¾in) tall

Needles:

1 pair 3.25mm (UK 10, US 3) knitting needles

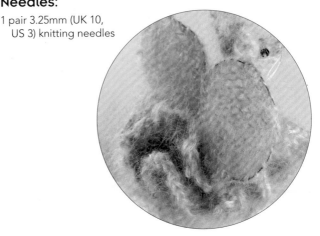

Instructions:

Tutu:

Using pink 4 ply yarn cast on 22 sts.

K 1 row.

Next row: Kfb into every st (44 sts).

K 1 row.

Rep these last 2 rows twice more (176 sts).

Cast off all sts.

Wings (make two):

Using fine cream yarn, cast on 3 sts.

Next row: K1, M1, K to last st, M1, K1 (5 sts).

K 1 row.

Rep the last 2 rows once more (9 sts).

K 6 rows.

Next row: K2tog, K to last 2 sts, K2tog (7 sts).

K 1 row.

Rep the last 2 rows until 3 sts rem.

Cast off.

Wand:

Take a length of fine wire, fold it in half and wrap with silver lurex yarn, as shown in the picture (right). Sew the button on to the end of the wand.

Making up:

Wrap the tutu twice round the mouse. Sew each end of the tutu together, securing it to the mouse. Take a length of fine wire and using the same yarn as for the wings, oversew the wire on to the edge of each wing, as shown above, leaving a length to tuck behind the tutu. Attach the wings. Sew the wand to the mouse's hand using the sewing needle.

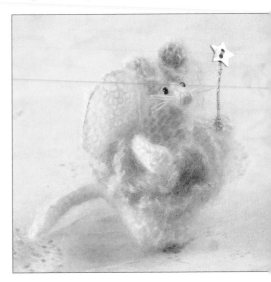

Festive Fairies

Turn a plain Christmas Mouse into a fairy with the addition of a knitted tutu, wings and a tiny but very magical wand.

Stocking

Materials:

Red 4 ply yarn
Small amount of cream and gold 4 ply yarn
Toy filling

Needles:

1 pair 3.25mm (UK 10, US 3)
  knitting needles
3.25mm crochet hook (optional)

Measurements:

Approx. 6.5cm (2½in) tall

Instructions:

Stocking:

Using red yarn, cast on 12 sts.

Row 1 (WS): P5, PM, P2, PM, P5.

Row 2: Cast on 4 sts, K to M, M1, SM, K2, SM, M1, K to end of row (18 sts).

Row 3: Cast on 4 sts, P to M, M1, SM, P2, SM, M1, P to end of row (24 sts).

Row 4: Cast on 6 sts, K to M, M1, SM, K2, SM, M1, K to end of row (32 sts).

Row 5: Cast on 6 sts, P to M, M1, SM, P2, SM, M1, P to end of row (40 sts).

Row 6: K to M, M1, SM, K2, SM, M1, K to end of row (42 sts).

Starting with a P row, work 3 rows in SS.

Next row: K to 2 sts before M, ssk, SM, K2, SM, K2tog, K to end of row (40 sts).

Next row: P to 2 sts before M, ssp, SM, P2, SM, P2tog, P to end of row (38 sts).

Rep the last 2 rows six more times until 26 sts rem.

Remove markers and work 12 rows in SS.

Change to cream and work 11 rows in GS.

Change to gold yarn and K1 row.

Cast off as follows (picot cast off):

* Cast on 2 sts, cast off 5 sts, pass st back to left-hand needle. Rep from * to the last 2 sts, cast off these sts. Fasten off yarn.

Hanging loop:

Using the crochet hook and cream yarn, make 12 chain sts. Fasten off. Alternatively, plait a length of yarn to make the loop.

Making up:

Sew the stocking's side seam, bearing in mind that the GS top will fold over so the WS will show. Sew in the ends. Attach the hook inside the stocking at the back after folding the top over. Stuff a little toy filling into the stocking.

A Very Mini Christmas!

These tiny stockings make perfect tree decorations, or you could put them out as table presents, filled with miniature gifts.

Holly Garland

Materials:

35mm (1³/₈in) curtain ring
Small amount of chunky yarn
Brown, green and red 4 ply yarn

Red beads and
    sewing thread
Sewing needle

Needles:

1 pair 2.75mm (UK 12, US 2)
    knitting needles

Instructions:

Garland:

Using the brown 4 ply yarn, cast on 14 sts.

* Work 4 rows in SS.

Next row (RS): K10, W&T.

Next row: P6, W&T.

Next row: K to end of row.

P 1 row.

Rep from * until the knitted strip is long
enough to wrap around the curtain ring. Cast
off on a K row.

Holly leaves (make 9):

Using green 4 ply, cast on 3 sts and work 2 rows
in SS.

* Next row: Kfb three times (6 sts).

Next row: P3, M1, P3 (7 sts).

Next row: Cast off 2 sts, K to end of row (5 sts).

Next row: Cast off 2 sts, P to end of row (3 sts).

Rep from * once more.

K 1 row.

Sl1, P2tog, psso. Fasten off rem st.

Measurements:

Approx 8cm (3¹/₈in) diameter

Bow:

Using red 4 ply, cast on 6 sts, working in GS
until the bow measures 7cm (2¾in). Join cast on
and cast off edges together. Fold flat, placing
the join at the back and sew together.

Cast on 3 sts to make the tie and work 2cm
(¾in) in GS. Cast off and attach to make the
bow centre, pulling tightly (see picture).

Make the bow tails by casting on 4 sts and
working 2.5cm (1in) in GS. Cast off and attach
to the back of the bow at an angle.

Making up:

To 'pad' the curtain ring, wrap with the chunky
yarn. Sew the brown garland piece around the
ring, joining the seam in the centre of the ring.
Sew the bow on to the garland at the top of
the curtain ring. Sew the holly leaves in place.
Sew beads on to the holly leaves using the
sewing thread and sewing needle.

Dinky Decoration

This alternative is made with pale grey and silver lurex 4 ply yarn
and creates a sparkling, frosted look if you are taking a break
from red and green this year.

Sweetie Cone

Materials:

Small amounts of cream,
red, green and gold
4 ply yarn

Gold beads

Felt for lining

Sewing needle and thread

Needles:

1 pair 3.25mm (UK 10, US 3)
knitting needles

Measurements:

Approx. 10cm (4in) from point to
rim of cone

Instructions:

The cone is worked in SS throughout.

Using cream yarn, cast on 5 sts and work 2 rows
in SS.

Next row: (K1, M1) four times, K1 (9 sts).

Work 2 rows.

Change to red and P 1 row.

Next row: (K2, M1) four times, K1 (13 sts).

Work 3 rows.

Next row: K2, (M1, K3) three times, M1, K2
(17 sts).

P 1 row.

Change to gold yarn and K1 row. Change back
to red yarn, P1 row.

Next row: K3, (M1, K4) three times, M1, K2
(21 sts).

Work 2 rows. Change to cream yarn and P 1 row.

Next row: K3, (M1, K5) three times, M1, K3
(25 sts).

P1 row. Change to green yarn, work 2 rows.

Next row: K3, (M1, K4) five times, M1, K2 (31 sts).

P 1 row. Change to gold yarn and K 1 row.

Change to green yarn and work 2 rows.

Change to red yarn and P 1 row.

Next row: K4 (M1, K5) five times, M1, K2 (37 sts).

P1 row.

Change to cream yarn and work 2 rows.

Change to red yarn and work 2 rows.

Cast off using a picot cast off as follows:

* Cast on 2 sts, cast off 5 sts, sl st from right-
hand to left-hand needle. Rep from * until 1 st
remains, cast off last st. Once you have cast off,
thread the tail of the yarn through the cast off
sts on the inside of the cone to pull the picot
edge in and make it stand up straight, as the
picot cast off will be wider than the SS cone.

Making up:

Before sewing up, use the knitted cone as a
pattern to cut out a piece of felt to line the
cone. Carefully sew up the side of the cone
using mattress stitch (see page 6), being careful
to match stripes. Twist the felt lining into a cone
shape and place it inside the knitted cone. Sew
the top edge of the lining to the top edge of
the cone to secure it. Thread approximately 9
beads on to a length of cream yarn and attach
the yarn in a loop at the bottom of the cone,
using the picture as a guide. Thread beads on
to a length of yarn and secure each end inside
the top edge of the cone to make a handle.

Sparkling Treats

This frosty looking alternative is made from pale grey, sparkly white,
blue and silver lurex yarn, with silver beads. There are white and silver
sweets inside for comfort on icy days.

Fir Tree Egg Cosy

Materials:

White sparkly 4 ply yarn

Small amount of silver 4 ply yarn

Silver beads (I used 31) and
white sewing thread

Sewing needle

Toy filling

Needles:

1 pair 2.75mm (UK 12, US
2) and 1 pair 4mm (UK 8,
US 6) knitting needles

Measurements:

Approx. 8cm (3¹⁄₈in) tall

Instructions:

Egg cosy:

Using a double strand of white yarn and 4mm
(UK 8, US 6) knitting needles, cast on 32 sts.

Work 2 rows in GS. Starting with a P row, work
11 rows in SS.

Next row: K3, (K2tog, K4) to last 5 sts, K2tog, K3
(27 sts).

P 1 row.

K2, (K2tog, K3) to end of row (22 sts).

P 1 row.

Next row: (K1, K2tog) to last st, K1 (15 sts).

P 1 row.

Next row: K2tog to last st, K1 (8 sts).

Cut yarn, thread yarn through rem sts and use
length of yarn to sew the side seam up.

Leaves:

The leaves are worked in strips of triangles in
the following way:

Using 2.75mm (UK 12, US 2) knitting needles
and MC, cast on 4 sts.

* K1 row.

K4, M1 (5 sts).

K 1 row.

K5, M1 (6 sts).

K 1 row.

K6, M1 (7 sts).

K 1 row.

K5, K2tog (6 sts).

K 1 row.

K4, K2tog (5 sts).

K 1 row.

K3, K2tog (4 sts).

These instructions make one 'point'. Repeat
from * until the length of points goes around
the bottom edge of the egg cosy.

Make five lengths of points: three lengths of
7 points, one of 6 points and one of 4 points.
Measure as you go as you may have to adjust
these numbers to fit your egg cosy.

Bobble:

Using silver yarn and 2.75mm (UK 12, US 2)
knitting needles, cast on 5 sts.

K 1 row.

P1, M1, P3, M1, P1 (7 sts).

Work six rows in SS.

Next row: K2tog at beginning and end of row.

Cast off rem sts.

Making up:

Sew strips of leaves on to the cosy, overlapping slightly and offsetting the points on each layer. For the top section of leaves, run a length of yarn along the top edge, gather and sew on to the top of the cosy. Run a length of yarn around the edges of the bobble, fill it with a small amount of toy filling and sew it to the top of the cosy. Using a sewing needle and white thread, sew a bead on to each point, using the picture as a guide.

Christmas Breakfast
What could be nicer before all that festive food, than a simple egg in a beautiful egg cosy, shown here in more traditional colours?

Rudolph

Materials:

Brown 4 ply yarn

Small amounts of cream, dark brown, black and red 4 ply yarn

1cm (³⁄₈in) bell

Toy filling

Needles:

1 pair 2.75mm (UK 12, US 2) knitting needles (double-pointed needles recommended)

2.75mm crochet hook (optional)

Measurements:

Approx. 9cm (3½in) nose to tail

Instructions:

Body:

Using brown 4 ply, cast on 14 sts, P 1 row.

Work inc rows as follows:

K1, (K1fb, K1, K1fb) to last st, K1. P 1 row (22 sts).

K1, (K1fb, K3, K1fb) to last st, K1. P 1 row (30 sts).

K1, (K1fb, K5, K1fb) to last st, K1. P 1 row (38 sts).

K1, (K1fb, K7, K1fb) to last st, K1. P 1 row (46 sts).

K1, (K1fb, K9, K1fb) to last st, K1. P 1 row (54 sts).

Work 10 rows in SS.

Work dec rows as follows:

K1, (K2tog, K9, ssk) to last st, K1. P 1 row (46 sts).

K1, (K2tog, K7, ssk) to last st, K1. P 1 row (38 sts).

K1, (K2tog, K5, ssk) to last st, K1. P 1 row (30 sts).

K1, (K2tog, K3, ssk) to last st, K1. P 1 row (22 sts).

K1, (K2tog, K1, ssk) to last st, K1. P 1 row (14 sts).

Thread yarn through rem sts, fasten off.

Head:

Using brown 4 ply, cast on 14 sts, P 1 row.

Work inc rows as follows:

K1, (K1fb, K1, K1fb) to last st, K1. P 1 row (22 sts).

K1, (K1fb, K3, K1fb) to last st, K1. P 1 row (30 sts).

Work 8 rows in SS.

Change to cream 4 ply and work dec rows as follows:

K1, (K2tog, K3, ssk) to last st, K1. P 1 row (22 sts).

K1, (K2tog, K1, ssk) to last st, K1. P 1 row (14 sts).

Thread yarn through rem sts. Fasten off.

Bobble (nose):

Using red yarn, cast on 1 st.

Next row: knit into the front, back and front of the st (3 sts).

Starting with a K row, work 3 rows in SS.

Next row: sl1, K2tog, psso (1 st). Run a length of yarn around the edges of the bobble, leaving a tail to attach to the head.

Antlers (make two):

Using dark brown yarn, cast on 3 sts and work an i-cord 4cm (1⁵⁄₈in) long (see page 6). Thread yarn through sts and fasten off. Make two more i-cords in this way, one 2.5cm (1in) long and another 1.5cm (⁵⁄₈in) long.

Legs (make four):

Using black yarn, cast on 4 sts and work 2 rows using the i-cord technique. Change to MC and continue until the leg measures 4cm (1⅝in). Thread yarn through sts and fasten off.

Ears (make two):

Using brown yarn, cast on 3 sts, starting with a K row, work 4 rows in SS.

Next row: sl1, K2tog, psso.

Fasten off rem st.

Tail:

Using MC, cast on 7 sts, cast off.

Collar:

Using the 2.75mm crochet hook, work a chain long enough to go around the reindeer's neck. Fasten off. Alternatively, plait a length of yarn to make the collar.

Making up:

Sew the head and body seams, stuffing as you close. Attach the head to the body, using the picture as a guide. Attach the legs, tail and ears. To make the antlers, sew the shorter i-cords to the longer i-cord. Sew in the ends. Sew the antlers to the head, behind the ears. Sew the bobble to the centre of head for the nose. Using black yarn, embroider the eyes. Sew the collar in place and attach the bell.

Frosty the Red-Nosed Reindeer

This alternative reindeer is made from pale grey, blue, sparkly white and red yarn, a very magical companion to the more natural-coloured Rudolph.

31

Snowman

Materials:

White sparkly 4 ply yarn

Small amounts of brown, green,
   black and orange 4 ply yarn

Self-patterning 4 ply yarn for scarf

Toy filling

Needles:

1 pair 2.75mm (UK 12,
   US 2) knitting needles
   (double-pointed needles
   recommended)

Measurements:

Approx. 8cm (3⅛in) tall

Instructions:

Body:

Using white sparkly 4 ply yarn, cast on 14 sts,
P 1 row.

Work increase rows as follows:

K1, (K1fb, K1, K1fb) to last st, K1. P 1 row
(22 sts).

K1, (K1fb, K3, K1fb) to last st, K1. P 1 row
(30 sts).

K1, (K1fb, K5, K1fb) to last st, K1. P 1 row
(38 sts).

K1, (K1fb, K7, K1fb) to last st, K1. P 1 row
(46 sts).

K1, (K1fb, K9, K1fb) to last st, K1. P 1 row
(54 sts).

Work 2 rows in SS. Work decrease rows as
follows:

K1, (K2tog, K9, ssk) to last st, K1. P1 row (46 sts).

K1, (K2tog, K7, ssk) to last st, K1. P1 row (38 sts).

K1, (K2tog, K5, ssk) to last st, K1. P1 row (30 sts).

K1, (K2tog, K3, ssk) to last st, K1. P1 row (22 sts).

K1, (K2tog, K1, ssk) to last st, K1. P1 row (14 sts).

Thread yarn through rem sts and fasten off.

Head:

Using white sparkly 4 ply yarn, cast on 14 sts,
P 1 row.

Work inc rows as follows:

K1, (K1fb, K1, K1fb) to last st, K1. P 1 row
(22 sts).

K1, (K1fb, K3, K1fb) to last st, K1. P 1 row
(30 sts).

K1, (K1fb, K5, K1fb) to last st, K1. P 1 row
(38 sts).

K1, (K1fb, K7, K1fb) to last st, K1. P 1 row
(46 sts).

Work decrease rows as follows:

K1, (K2tog, K7, ssk) to last st, K1. P 1 row (38 sts).

K1, (K2tog, K5, ssk) to last st, K1. P 1 row (30 sts).

K1, (K2tog, K3, ssk) to last st, K1. P 1 row (22 sts).

K1, (K2tog, K1, ssk) to last st, K1. P 1 row (14 sts).

Thread yarn through rem sts and fasten off.

Nose:

Using orange 4 ply yarn, cast on 5 sts.

P 1 row.

K2tog, K1, K2tog (3 sts).

Sl1, K2tog, psso.

Fasten off rem st.

Hat:

Using green 4 ply yarn, cast on 5 sts.

Next row: K1, (M1, K1) to last st, M1, K1 (9 sts).

P 1 row.

Rep the last 2 rows twice more (33 sts).

P 1 row (RS).

Starting with a P row, work 7 rows in SS.

Next row: (K2, M1) to last st, K1 (49 sts).

P 1 row.

Work 3 rows in GS. Cast off.

Making up:

Stuff and sew the side seams of the body and head. Attach the head to the body. Sew on the arms. Sew the side seam of the hat and sew it on to the snowman's head. Sew up the nose and attach. Using French knots, embroider the eyes and buttons with black 4 ply yarn and a darning needle. Tie the scarf around the snowman's neck.

Arms (make two):

Using brown 4 ply, cast on 4 sts and work an i-cord 2.5cm (1in) long (see page 6). Work a second i-cord just 0.5cm (¼in) long and sew it on to the first i-cord to make a 'forked' hand.

Scarf:

Using 4 ply yarn, cast on 7 sts and work 10cm (4in) in GS. Cast off.

White Christmas

This snowman has a cool blue look with his colour-coordinated hat and scarf set. You can use up your odds and ends of yarn dressing up these snowmen, as long as you have enough white!

Rocking Robin

Materials:

Small amounts of brown, cream, red, dark grey and orange 4 ply yarn

Toy filling

Measurements:

Approx. 6cm (2³⁄₈in) diameter body

Needles:

1 pair 2.75mm (UK 12, US 2) knitting needles (double-pointed needles recommended)

Instructions:

Body:

Using cream yarn, cast on 14 sts, P 1 row.

Work inc rows as follows:

K1, (K1fb, K1, K1fb) to last st, K1. P 1 row (22 sts).

K1, (K1fb, K3, K1fb) to last st, K1. P 1 row (30 sts).

K1, (K1fb, K5, K1fb) to last st, K1. P 1 row (38 sts).

K1, (K1fb, K7, K1fb) to last st, K1. P 1 row (46 sts).

K1, (K1fb, K9, K1fb) to last st, K1. P 1 row (54 sts).

K1, (K1fb, K11, K1fb) to last st, K1. P 1 row (62 sts).

Work 2 rows in SS. Change to brown and work 4 rows in SS.

Work dec rows as follows:

K1, (K2tog, K11, ssk) to last st, K1. P 1 row (54 sts).

K1, (K2tog, K9, ssk) to last st, K1. P 1 row (46 sts).

K1, (K2tog, K7, ssk) to last st, K1. P 1 row (38 sts).

K1, (K2tog, K5, ssk) to last st, K1. P 1 row (30 sts).

K1, (K2tog, K3, ssk) to last st, K1. P 1 row (22 sts).

K1, (K2tog, K1, ssk) to last st, K1. P 1 row (14 sts).

Thread yarn through rem sts and fasten off.

Red breast:

Using red yarn, cast on 14 sts and work 2 rows in SS.

Next row: K1, M1, K to last st, M1, K1. P 1 row.

Rep these 2 rows once more (18 sts).

Work 4 rows in SS.

Next row: K7, ssk, K2tog, K7 (16 sts). P 1 row.

Rep the last 2 rows, working 2 less st before and after dec shapings until 6 sts rem.

Work 4 rows in SS.

Next row: ssk, K2, K2tog.

Cast off rem 4 sts (WS).

Beak:

Using orange yarn, cast on 5 sts and P 1 row.

Next row: ssk, K1, K2tog. Thread yarn through resulting 3 sts and sew seam.

Wings (make two):

Using brown yarn, cast on 10 sts and work 2 rows in SS.

Next row: K1, M1, K to last st, M1, K1 (12 sts).

P 1 row. Rep these 2 rows once more (14 sts).

Work 2 rows in SS.

Next row: K1, ssk, K to last 3 sts, K2tog, K1 (12 sts).

P 1 row.

Rep the last 2 rows until 4 sts rem.

Next row: ssk, K2tog (3 sts).

K2tog and fasten off rem st.

Tail:

Using brown yarn, cast on 7 sts and work in rib as follows:

Row 1: K1, P1 three times, K1.

Row 2: P1, K1 three times, P1.

Work a further 6 rows in K1, P1 rib.

Next row: K1, K2tog, P1, K2tog, K1 (5 sts).

Work 1 row as set in rib.

Next row: ssk, P1, K2tog (3 sts).

Work 1 row in rib and cast off rem sts.

Making up:

Sew the side seam of the body and stuff it with toy filling without distorting the shape. Sew the breast on to the front of the body with the RS showing, using the picture as a guide. Embroider the eyes using black yarn and attach the beak. Lightly press the wings and sew them on to the body at an angle. Sew the foot to the bottom of the leg. Repeat for the second leg and sew the legs on to the body.

Legs (make two):

Using dark grey yarn, cast on 4 sts and work an 'i-cord' (see page 6) 4cm (1⁵⁄₈in) long. Thread yarn through sts and fasten.

Feet (make two):

Each foot consists of three 'toes'. To make each toe, cast on 4 sts using dark grey yarn and work 4 rows of 'i-cord'. Thread yarn through sts and fasten. Sew the three toes together.

Frosty Friend

Robins have always featured on Christmas cards and they cheer up any winter scene. The alternative bird has a silver beak and legs with soft pink and grey feathers, and would tone in with sparkling, frosty-themed festivities.

Christmas Pud

Materials:

Small amounts of self-patterning, red, green, black and white 4 ply yarn

Stitch holder (or spare knitting needle)

Toy filling

Needles:

1 pair 2.75mm (UK 12, US 2) knitting needles

Measurements:

Approx. 6cm (2³⁄₈in) in diameter

Instructions:

Pudding:

Using self-patterning yarn, cast on 14 sts, P 1 row.

Work inc rows as follows:

K1, (K1fb, K1, K1fb) to last st, K1. P 1 row (22 sts).

K1, (K1fb, K3, K1fb) to last st, K1. P 1 row (30 sts).

K1, (K1fb, K5, K1fb) to last st, K1. P 1 row (38 sts).

K1, (K1fb, K7, K1fb) to last st, K1. P 1 row (46 sts).

K1, (K1fb, K9, K1fb) to last st, K1. P 1 row (54 sts).

K1, (K1fb, K11, K1fb) to last st, K1. P 1 row (62 sts).

Work 6 rows in SS. Work dec rows as follows:

K1, (K2tog, K11, ssk) to last st, K1. P1 row (54 sts).

K1, (K2tog, K9, ssk) to last st, K1. P 1 row (46 sts).

K1, (K2tog, K7, ssk) to last st, K1. P 1 row (38 sts).

K1, (K2tog, K5, ssk) to last st, K1. P 1 row (30 sts).

K1, (K2tog, K3, ssk) to last st, K1. P 1 row (22 sts).

K1, (K2tog, K1, ssk) to last st, K1. P 1 row (14 sts).

Thread yarn through rem sts and fasten.

Small icing drips (make three):

Using white sparkly yarn, cast on 2 sts.

Work 2 rows in SS.

Cut yarn and place sts on a st holder or spare needle.

Large icing drips (make two):

Using sparkly yarn, cast on 3 sts. P 1 row.

Next row: K1, M1, K1, M1, K1 (5 sts).

P 1 row.

Cut yarn and place sts on a st holder or spare needle.

Icing top:

Using white sparkly yarn, cast on as follows:

Cast on 6 sts, turn work and knit across 5 sts of large icing drip.

Turn work and cast on 6 sts, turn again and knit across 2 sts of small icing drip.

Turn work and cast on 10 sts, turn again and work across 2 sts of small icing drip.

Turn work and cast on 3 sts, turn work and knit across 5 sts of large icing drip.

Turn work and cast on 10 sts, turn work and knit across 2 sts of small icing drip. Turn work and cast on 3sts (54 sts).

P 1 row.

K1, (K2tog, K9, ssk) to last st, K1. P 1 row (46 sts).

K1, (K2tog, K7, ssk) to last st, K1. P 1 row (38 sts).

K1, (K2tog, K5, ssk) to last st, K1. P 1 row (30 sts).

K1, (K2tog, K3, ssk) to last st, K1. P 1 row (22 sts).

K1, (K2tog, K1, ssk) to last st, K1. P 1 row (14 sts).

Thread yarn through rem sts and fasten.

Holly leaves

Using green 4 ply, make three holly leaves following the pattern on page 24.

Making up:

Sew the side seam of the pudding and stuff it with toy filling without distorting the shape. Sew the seam of the icing and sew it on top of the pudding. Sew on the holly leaves, taking care to stitch the points on the leaves evenly. Embroider French knots in red in the centre of the leaves, and in black over the pudding for raisins, using the picture as a guide.

Perfect Puds

The other pudding is made from dark brown and cream yarn and has red beads sewn on for holly berries. Both make wonderful woolly baubles for the tree.

Christmas Angel

Materials:

Blue 4 ply yarn

Small amount of cream and silver lurex 4 ply yarn

Fine cream yarn (laceweight)

Small amount of pink and blue embroidery thread and embroidery needle

Fine wire

Toy filling

Needles:

1 pair 2.75mm (UK 12, US 2) double-pointed knitting needles recommended)

Measurements:

Approx. 9cm (3½in) tall from top of head to bottom of dress

Instructions:

Head:

Using cream 4 ply yarn cast on 14 sts, P 1 row.

Work inc rows as follows:

K1, (K1fb, K1, K1fb) to last st, K1. P 1 row (22 sts).

K1, (K1fb, K3, K1fb) to last st, K1. P 1 row (30 sts).

Work 4 rows in SS. Work dec rows as follows:

K1, (K2tog, K3, ssk) to last st, K1. P 1 row (22 sts).

K1, (K2tog, K1, ssk) to last st, K1. P 1 row (14 sts).

Thread yarn through rem sts, fasten.

Dress:

Using blue 4 ply yarn cast on 30 sts.

Work picot edging as follows:

K1, (cast off 2 sts, K2) five times, cast off 2 sts, K1 (18 sts).

P1 row.

Next row: K3, (M1, K4) three times, M1, K3 (22 sts).

P1 row.

Next row: K3, (M1, K4) four times, M1, K3 (27 sts).

P1 row.

Next row: K3, (M1, K4) five times, M1, K3, M1, K1 (34 sts).

P1 row.

Next row: K3, (M1, K5) five times, M1, K4, M1, K2 (41 sts).

P1 row.

Work lace edging as follows:

Next row: K2, *(K2tog) four times, (K1, YO) four times. Rep from * three times. K3.

K 3 rows.

Rep these 4 rows twice more. Cast off.

Sleeves:

Using blue 4 ply yarn, cast on 20 sts. K 2 rows.

Starting with a K row, continue in SS for 4 rows.

Next row: K1, K2tog, K to last 3 sts, ssk, K1 (18 sts).

P 1 row.

Rep the last 2 rows a further three times until you have 12 sts left.

K 2 rows. Cast off.

Wings (make two):

Using fine cream yarn, cast on 5 sts.

K 2 rows.

Next row: K1, M1, to last st, M1, K1 (7 sts).

K 1 row.

Rep these 2 rows three more times (13 sts).

K 6 rows.

Next row: K2tog, K to last 2 sts, K2tog (11 sts).

K 1 row.

Rep the last 2 rows three more times until 5 sts rem.

Cast off.

Legs (make two):

Using cream yarn, cast on 4 sts. Work an i-cord (see page 6) 9cm (3½in) long, or adjust the length so that the legs show beneath the dress.

Arms (make two):

Using cream yarn, cast on 4 sts. Work an i-cord long enough to stick out of the sleeves.

Making up:

Stuff and sew up the head. Embroider French knots on to the head to make hair using silver lurex yarn. Embroider the eyes and a mouth using embroidery thread. Attach the legs to the bottom of the head. Lightly press the dress as the shape will distort slightly when you work the lace edging. Sew up the back seam of the dress and gather it at the top, then sew it to the base of the head. Sew up the sleeve seams, attaching the arms as you go. Using the laceweight yarn, oversew a length of fine wire to the edges of the wings. Tuck the wire inside the dress at the back of the angel's head and sew the wings in place. Bend a length of wire into a halo shape and wrap it in silver lurex yarn. Attach it to the angel's head.

Treetop Angel

Knit your own heavenly host, changing the colours to suit your Christmas colour scheme.

What a Hoot

Materials:

Brown chunky yarn

Small amounts of beige, brown, red, cream and gold coloured 4 ply yarn

Gold lurex 4 ply yarn

Toy filling

Small brass bell

Two buttons and matching thread

Sewing needle

Needles:

1 pair 2.75mm (UK 12, US 2) and 1 pair 4.5mm (UK 7, US 7) knitting needles

Measurements: Approx. 10cm (4in) tall

Instructions:

Body (make two):

Using 4.5mm (UK 7, US 7) needles and chunky yarn, cast on 12 sts and work 2 rows in SS.

Next row: K1, M1, K to last st, M1, K1 (14 sts).

P 1 row.

Rep last 2 rows once more (16 sts).

Continue in SS for 10 rows.

Next row: K1, ssk, K to last 3 sts, K2tog, K1 (14 sts).

P 1 row.

Rep these 2 rows once more (12 sts).

Work 2 rows in SS.

Next row: K1, ssk, K to last 3 sts, K2tog, K1 (10 sts).

Next row: P4, cast off 2 sts, P to end of row (8 sts).

Turn and working on the first 4 sts, K1, ssk, K1 (3 sts).

P 1 row.

Next row: sl1, K2tog, psso. Fasten off rem st.

With RS facing, rejoin yarn to rem 4 sts, K1, K2tog, K1 (3 sts).

P 1 row.

Next row: sl1, K2tog, psso. Fasten off rem st.

Base:

Using 4.5mm (UK 7, US 7) needles and chunky yarn, cast on 3 sts. Work 2 rows in SS.

Next row: K1, M1, K1, M1, K1 (5 sts).

P 1 row.

Rep the last 2 rows once more (7 sts).

Work 2 rows in SS.

Next row: K1, ssk, K1, K2tog, K1 (5 sts).

P 1 row.

Next row: K1, ssk, K2tog, K1 (3 sts).

P 1 row (3 sts).

Cast off rem sts.

Tummy:

Using gold 4 ply yarn and 2.75mm (UK 12, US 2) knitting needles, cast on 10 sts, P 1 row.

Next row: K1, M1, K to last st, M1, K1 (12 sts).

P 1 row.

Rep the last 2 rows twice more (16 sts).

Work 4 rows in SS.

Next row: K6, ssk, K2tog, K6 (14 sts).

P 1 row.

Rep the last 2 rows, working one less st before and after decreases until 6 sts rem. Cast off rem sts.

Eyes:

Cast on 4 sts using beige 4 ply yarn and 2.75mm (UK 12, US 2) knitting needles. P 1 row.

Next row: K1, M1, K2, M1, K1 (6 sts).

P 1 row.

Work in SS for 4 rows.

Next row: ssk, K2, K2tog (4 sts).

P 1 row. Cast off rem sts.

Beak:

Cast on 5 sts using gold lurex yarn and 2.75mm (UK 12, US 2) needles and work 2 rows in SS.

Next row: K2tog, K1, K2tog. P 1 row.

Thread yarn through rem 3 sts and sew up seam of beak.

Wings:

Cast on 3 sts using brown 4 ply yarn and 2.75mm (UK 12, US 2) knitting needles.

The wings are worked in GS throughout.

K 2 rows.

Next row: K1, M1, K to end of row (4 sts).

K 1 row.

Rep the last 2 rows until you have 8 sts.

Knit 12 rows.

Next row: K1, K2tog, K to last 3 sts, K2tog, K1.

K 1 row.

Rep the last 2 rows until 4 sts rem.

Next row: K2tog twice, cast off rem st and fasten off yarn.

Hat:

Using 2.75mm (UK 12, US 2) needles and cream 4 ply, cast on 22 sts and work 12 rows in GS.

Change to red 4 ply.

Work 8 rows in SS.

Next row: (K1, K2tog) seven times, K1 (15 sts).

P 1 row.

Next row: (K1, K2tog) to end of row (10 sts).

P 1 row.

Work 2 rows in SS.

Next row: K2tog to end of row (5 sts).

P 1 row.

Thread yarn through rem sts, sew up side seam of hat, pulling the yarn slightly as you sew so the top of the hat folds over slightly. Fold GS edging up.

Making up:

Sew up the side seams and stuff the owl with toy filling. Sew in the base, adding a piece of card to strengthen it if required. Attach the tummy, beak, wings and knitted eyes. Using a sewing needle and matching thread, sew on buttons for eyes. Attach the bell to the top of the hat.

French Hen

Materials:

Small amount of chunky yarn

Small amounts of red, orange, black and self-patterning 4 ply yarn

Two stitch holders

Toy filling

Needles:

1 pair 4.5mm (UK 7, US 7) and 1 pair 2.75mm (UK 12, US 2) knitting needles

Measurements:

Approx. 10cm (4in) tall

Instructions:

Body:

Using chunky yarn and 4.5mm (UK 7, US 7) knitting needles, cast on 31 sts.

Next row: (K4, M1) seven times, K3 (38 sts).

P 1 row. Continue in SS until work measures 6cm (2³⁄₈in).

Next row: K5 and turn, placing rem sts on a holder. P 1 row.

You are now working the tail.

Next row: K3, K2tog (4 sts).

Next row: P2, P2tog (3 sts) K 1 row.

Next row: sl1, P2tog, psso. Fasten off rem st.

With WS facing, rejoin yarn to opposite end of the row, P5 and turn (second half of tail).

Next row: K2tog, K3 (4 sts).

Next row: P2tog, P2 (3 sts). K 1 row.

Next row: sl1, K2tog, psso. Fasten off rem st.

28 sts remain. Shape head as follows:

With RS facing, slip rem 6 sts on to holder and rejoin yarn. K across next 16 sts, sl rem 6 sts on to a holder.

Next row: P7, PM, P2, PM, P7.

Next row: K2tog, K to last 2 sts, SM, K2tog. P1 row (14 sts).

Next row: K2tog, K4, M1, SM, K2, SM, M1, K4, K2tog (14 sts).

Next row: P6, M1, SM, P2, SM, M1, P6 (16 sts).

Next row: K7, M1, SM, K2, SM, M1, K7 (18 sts).

Remove markers. You will now be working on one side of the head.

Next row: P2tog, P5, P2tog, turn work leaving rem 9 sts on your needle.

** Next row: K2tog, K3, K2tog.

P2tog, P1, P2tog. Cast off rem 3 sts.

With WS facing, rejoin yarn to held sts and work as follows:

P2tog, P5, P2tog. Work from ** to end.

Cast off the rem 12 sts.

Wings (make two):

Using chunky yarn and 4.5mm (UK 7, US 7) needles, cast on 5 sts, K 1 row.

Row 1: K1, M1, K to last st, M1, K1 (7 sts).

K 1 row.

Rep these 2 rows twice more (11 sts).

K 1 row.

Next row: K2tog, K to last 2 sts, K2tog (9sts).

Next row: K to last 2 sts, K2tog (8 sts).

Cast off 2 sts, K to end (6 sts).

Next row: K2tog, K2, K2tog (4 sts).

Next row: K2tog, K to end of row (3 sts).

Cast off.

Base:

Using chunky yarn and 4.5mm (UK 7, US 7) needles, cast on 3 sts. K1, M1, K to last st, M1, K1 (5 sts).

P 1 row.

Rep these 2 rows a further three times (11 sts).

Continue in SS until work measures 4.5cm (1¾in).

Next row: K1, K2tog, K to last 3 sts, K2tog, K1.

P 1 row.

Rep last 2 rows until 5 sts rem.

Next row: K2tog, K1, K2tog. Cast off rem 3 sts.

Beak:

Using 2.75mm (UK 12, US 2) knitting needles and orange 4 ply, cast on 5 sts and P1 row.

K2tog, K1, K2tog (3 sts). P 1 row.

Thread yarn through rem sts and fasten off.

Comb:

Using red 4 ply and 2.75mm (UK 12, US 2) needles, cast on 2 sts, K 1 row.

M1, K2. K 1 row.

* Cast off 2 sts (1 st).

Next row: M1, K1. K 1 row.

Next row: M1, K2. K 1 row. Rep from * once more. Cast off.

Tail feathers (make five):

Using chunky yarn and 4.5mm (UK 7, US 7) knitting needles, cast on 6 sts, cast sts off.

Scarf:

Using self-patterning 4 ply yarn and 2.75mm (UK 12, US 2) knitting needles, cast on 7 sts. Work 20cm (7⅞in) in GS. Cast off and sew in the ends.

Making up:

Sew the seams of the body together. Stuff and sew on the base. You can cut a piece of card to fit inside the base to make it flat. Sew the seam of the beak and attach it. Sew the wings, comb and tail feathers in place using the pictures as a guide. Embroider the eyes using French knots.

Festive Farmyard

The cream-coloured hen wears a natty blue scarf. French hens feature in the Christmas song, but you could get these out again for Easter and surround them with little eggs.

Turtle Dove

Materials:

Red 4 ply yarn

Small amounts of cream, gold and black
   4 ply yarn

Toy filling

Needles:

1 pair 3.25mm (UK 10, US 3)
   knitting needles

Measurements:

Approx. 12cm (4¾in) from
   beak to tail

Instructions:

Body:

Using red 4 ply yarn, cast on 10 sts and work 6
rows in SS.

Next row: K4, PM, K2, PM, K4.

P 1 row.

Next row: K to M, M1, SM, K2, SM, M1, K to end
of row (12 sts).

P 1 row.

Rep the last 2 rows a further six times until
24 sts rem.

Work 2 rows in SS.

Next row: K to 2 sts before M, ssk, SM, K2, SM,
K2tog, K to end of row (22 sts).

P 1 row.

Rep the last 2 rows until 18 sts rem.

Next row: K1, M1, K to 2 sts before M, ssk, SM,
K2, SM, K2tog, K to last st, M1, K1 (18 sts).

Next row: P1, M1, P to 2 sts before M, ssp, SM,
P2, SM, P2togtbl, P to last st, M1, P1 (18 sts).

Next row: K to 2 sts before M, ssk, SM, K2,
SM, K2tog, K to end of row (16 sts).

P 1 row.

Next row: K1, ssk, K2, ssk, SM, K2, SM,
K2tog, K2, K2tog, K1 (12 sts).

P 1 row.

Change to gold yarn.

Next row: K2tog, rep to end of row (6 sts).

P 1 row.

Next row: K2tog, rep to end of row (3 sts).

Thread yarn through rem sts and
fasten off.

Tail feathers:

Make three of each in cream and gold.

Cast on 2 sts and K 8 rows.

Next row: K1, M1, K1 (3 sts).

K 12 rows.

Next row: sl1, K2tog, psso. Fasten off rem st.

Large feathers for wings:

Make four of each in cream and gold.

Cast on 2 sts and K 4 rows.

Next row: K1, M1, K1 (3 sts).

K 8 rows.

Next row: sl1, K2tog, psso. Fasten off rem st.

Small feathers for wings:

Make two in gold.

Cast on 2 sts and K 4 rows.

Next row: K1, M1, K1 (3 sts).

K 5 rows.

Next row: sl1, K2tog, psso. Fasten off rem st.

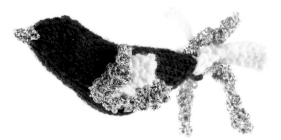

Making up:

Sew the seam of the bird, stuffing with toy filling as you go. Embroider a French knot on each side of the head for the eyes. Attach the tail feathers. Sew two larger feathers together and attach them to the sides of the bird. Sew the smaller feathers on top of the larger ones to shape the wings.

Two Turtle Doves

Sparkly white yarn with pale grey and blue makes a companion for the red turtle dove. They could sit together in your Christmas tree or table decoration.

Nordic Bunting

Materials:

Red 4 ply yarn

Small amount of cream 4 ply yarn

Needles:

1 pair 3.25mm (UK 10, US 3) knitting needles

3mm crochet hook (optional)

Measurements:

Each pennant approx. 11cm (4¼in) high and 7cm (2¾in) wide

Motifs:

The charts for the motifs are on page 7.

Instructions:

Using red 4 ply, cast on 1 st.

Next row: K into the front, back and front of the stitch (3sts).

Next row: K1, P1, K1.

Next row: K1, M1, P1, M1, K1 (5 sts).

Next row: K1, P1, K1, P1, K1.

Next row: K1, P1, M1, K1, M1, P1, K1 (7 sts).

Next row (RS): K1, P1, K3, P1, K1.

Next row: (K1, P1) three times, K1.

Continue as follows:

Row 1: **K1, P1, K1**, M1, work to last 3 sts, M1, **K1, P1, K1**.

Row 2: **K1, P1, K1**, work to last 3 sts, **K1, P1, K1**.

Keeping the 3 border sts in Moss st (marked in bold), work these 2 rows a further six times, inc either side of the central SS panel until you have 21 sts.

Work 2 rows with no further shaping.

Keeping Moss st edges, work 20 rows of your selected chart (see page 7).

Work a further 2 rows.

Work 4 rows in Moss st. Cast off all sts.

Making up:

Either sew the corners of the pennants together or crochet across the top of each pennant to join them together.

Yuletide Yarn

Deck your halls with this beautiful woollen bunting, shown here in cream with gold motifs.

Acknowledgements

Thank you to everyone who helped test knit and check these patterns and those who helped in other ways to enable me to finish on time: Lucy, Phyl, Bekky, Claire, Janet, Babs, Elaine, Karen, Jennie, Pippa, Alix, Andrea, Ailsa, and last but by no means least, Mark. Also, thanks to my family, for whom Christmas went on a bit longer than usual!

Publisher's Note

If you would like more information about
knitting, try the following books by Search Press:
Beginner's Guide to Knitting by Alison Dupernex, Search Press, 2004
and in the Twenty to Make series by Search Press:
Knitted Cakes by Susan Penny, 2008; *Knitted Flowers* by Susie Johns, 2010
Eco-Friendly Knits by Emily Blades, 2010; *Knitted Aliens* by Fiona McDonald, 2010
Knitted Bears by Val Pierce, 2010; *Knitted Mug Hugs* by Val Pierce, 2010
Knitted Vegetables by Susie Johns, 2011 and *Knitted Fruit* by Susie Johns, 2011